SEE-THROUGH
PIRATES

Kelly Davis

Ivy Press

First published in the UK in 2007 by
Ivy Press
The Old Candlemakers
West Street, Lewes
East Sussex, BN7 2NZ, UK
www.ivy-group.co.uk

Copyright © 2003 Ivy Press Limited

All rights reserved. No part of this publication may be reproduced or transmitted in any form or by any means, electronic or mechanical, including photocopying, recording, or by any information storage and retrieval system, without permission in writing from the publisher.

ISBN 10: 1-905695-35-7
ISBN 13: 978-1-905695-35-5

British Library Cataloguing-in-Publication Data. A catalogue record for this book is available from the British Library.

Ivy Press
This book was designed and produced by Ivy Press

PUBLISHER Alastair Campbell
EXECUTIVE PUBLISHER Sophie Collins
CREATIVE DIRECTOR Peter Bridgewater
EDITORIAL DIRECTOR Steve Luck
DESIGN MANAGER Tony Seddon
SENIOR PROJECT EDITOR Rebecca Saraceno
DESIGNER Kevin Knight
ILLUSTRATIONS
Julian Baker, Coral Mula
and Ivan Hissey

This book is based on an outline
by John Malam.

Printed in China

1 2 3 4 5 6 7 8 9 10

CONTENTS

WHEN PIRATES RULED THE WAVES ▲ 3

THE SPANISH MAIN ▲ 4

PIRATE ATTACK! ▲ 6

PIRATE CREW ▲ 10

LIFE AT A PIRATE HAVEN ▲ 12

PIRATE WEAPONS ▲ 16

PIRATE PUNISHMENTS ▲ 18

LIFE AT SEA ▲ 22

CAPTURE AND TRIAL ▲ 24

THE TRUE STORY OF THE WHYDAH ▲ 28

ROGUES' GALLERY ▲ 30

GLOSSARY / INDEX ▲ 32

WHEN PIRATES RULED THE WAVES

Pirates (or seafaring robbers) have existed ever since ancient peoples began trading goods. As early as 2000 BCE, the seafaring Phoenicians were using their ships for both trade and piracy. A few centuries later, Phoenician sailors carrying silver and amber across the Mediterranean Sea were themselves threatened by Greek pirates. And in the fourth century BCE the Greek emperor Alexander the Great was troubled by pirates on the Aegean Sea. Much later, Viking longships roamed northern Europe in search of plunder. And, from the Middle Ages onward, North African pirates (known as Barbary corsairs) attacked Italian merchant vessels. Pirates still exist today, particularly in Southeast Asia.

CHINESE PIRATES

From the early 1600s Chinese pirates preyed on European merchant ships in the Southeast Asian seas. These pirates sailed on "junks," wooden vessels with sails made of bamboo matting. On one occasion in 1849, a fleet of nearly 60 Chinese vessels was destroyed by the British Navy.

◁ **Under fire**
Chinese junks were armed with cannons, but they were no match for the British Navy's paddle steamers.

▷ **Anti-pirate patrols**
Rome sent *bireme* (meaning "two rows" of oarsmen) and sometimes *trireme* ("three-row") galleys to attack the pirates.

The eye symbol was believed to help the ship "see" its prey.

Roman galleys used the ram on their prows to sink enemy ships.

Rome's soldiers were well-armed, but still met fierce resistance from the pirates.

PIRATES IN ROMAN TIMES

The ancient Romans were great traders who depended on being able to transport food between different parts of their huge empire. But by the first century BCE, constant piracy was threatening Rome's supply of grain from Egypt. A general called Pompey the Great was sent to round up the pirates, while the Roman army attacked their base in Cilicia (modern southeastern Turkey). About 20,000 pirates were captured, 10,000 were killed, and Pompey was hailed as a hero. Nevertheless, pirates continued to loot Roman ships until the second century CE.

PIRATE POINTS

☠ **Julius Caesar was once kidnapped by pirates**
- In 78 BCE, the young Julius Caesar was held hostage by Cilician pirates on a tiny island.
- He was released after six weeks, when the ransom of 50 talents was paid.

THE SPANISH MAIN

Since Christopher Columbus's voyage to the New World in 1492 was financed by King Ferdinand of Spain, the Spanish were able to claim many lands in Central and South America. In 1503, the Pope granted ownership of this area to Spain and it became known as the Spanish Main. The Spanish began to plunder the vast wealth of the Aztec and Inca people and Spanish treasure fleets were soon crossing the Caribbean and the Atlantic, carrying valuable cargoes of gold and silver and offering easy prey for pirates. Thus the Spanish Main became the setting for a "Golden Age" of piracy, which reached its height between 1680 and 1730.

WHERE WAS THE SPANISH MAIN?
The Spanish Main originally meant the land stretching from the northern coast of South America to Florida in North America. Later it came to include the Caribbean and its islands, such as the Bahamas, Jamaica, Cuba, Hispaniola (modern Haiti), Tortuga, and the Windward Islands. The Spanish treasure fleets usually kept to the same routes in the Caribbean, making them easy to attack.

▷ **Ship ahoy!**
A lookout aboard a pirate sloop spots a Spanish fleet and alerts his fellow crew members.

A Spanish galleon laden with treasure from the New World.

STRENGTH IN NUMBERS?
Every year the Spanish sent two fleets to the Spanish Main. One fleet collected Aztec treasure from Vera Cruz in Mexico, and the other fleet went to Nombre de Dios in modern Panama to collect gold and silver brought from Peru and Ecuador. The two fleets, totalling around 100 ships, would then meet at Havana, in Cuba, to begin the long journey back to Spain. Although each galleon was armed with up to 60 cannons, they were still frequently overwhelmed by pirates.

PIRATE POINTS
☠ **More facts about Spanish treasure ships**
- The galleons had a large square sail on each mainmast. They only sailed well when the wind was behind them.
- Each ship had a crew of about 200 men.

FRANCIS DRAKE

FRANÇOIS L'OLONNAIS

BARTHOLOMEW ROBERTS

PRIVATEERS, PIRATES, AND BUCCANEERS
Privateers, like Francis Drake (ca.1543–1596), sailed privately owned ships, and their crews were legally authorized by Spain's enemies, such as the English, French, and Dutch governments, to raid Spanish vessels in wartime. Privateers had to give most of their loot to the governments who hired them. Pirates, like Bartholomew Roberts (see page 31), captured vessels illegally in war or peace. The early buccaneers were European and Caribbean outlaw adventurers who lived on the islands of Hispaniola, Jamaica, and Tortuga, hunting wild pigs. They later became pirates. By the 1660s, they were attacking Spanish galleons. François l'Olonnais (ca. 1620s–1668) was a particularly savage buccaneer.

PIRATE POINTS
The brutal habits of buccaneers
- Buccaneers got their name because local Arawak tribespeople taught them how to barbecue their meat on grills called *boucans*. They used the smelly hides of pigs to make their clothes.
- François l'Olonnais once cut out and gnawed the heart of a Spanish captive, warning the other prisoners they would suffer the same fate unless they gave him their treasure right away.

WHY BE A PIRATE?
By the early 1800s more than 2,000 pirates were reckoned to be operating in the Caribbean. Most of them were in their late twenties and were drawn to this dangerous life because of their hunger for treasure. Many of them came from poor backgrounds. They believed they could make a fortune from piracy and then retire wealthy.

Gold candlesticks
Engraved silver beaker
Jeweled cross
Money chest
Doubloon
Gold Aztec ornament

▷ **The pirate life**
Both men and women became pirates, leaving their families for a life of adventure at sea.

NEW WORLD WEALTH
The Spanish treasure fleet sailed annually from 1530 to 1735, laden with seemingly limitless riches from the New World. Solid gold Aztec jewelry was often crushed or melted down to make gold coins known as *doubloons*; and silver ore was mined in Peru and then made into *pesos* ("pieces of eight"), silver coins which could be torn into pieces to make smaller coins.

◁ **Rich pickings**
Wealthy passengers on the Spanish vessels offered additional loot for pirates, including fine jewelry and tableware.

THE SPANISH MAIN 5

PIRATE ATTACK!

Unlike the crews of warships, pirates in the Spanish Main never aimed to sink the ships they attacked. They wanted to take them as their own vessels, so they tried to keep any damage to a minimum. The pirates would lie in wait for their prey off the American coast, then sail in close, board the ship, persuade the crew to become pirates (killing them if they refused), and loot any treasure (both from the ship's hold and from any wealthy passengers who were on board). The captured ship would then either be sold or kept for the pirates' own use.

PIRATE POINTS

☠ **Dastardly tricks used by pirates**
- Pirates used a square sail to make the most of the wind when it was coming from behind their ships.
- Pirates sometimes flew false flags so that their victims would not realize that they were under attack until it was too late.

UNDER FIRE

Once the pirates had damaged the masts and sails of the Spanish ships, they were unable to sail out of danger. Many Spanish crews surrendered immediately but others tried to defend themselves. As a last resort, some captains scattered broken glass on the decks to make it harder for the barefoot pirates to board their vessels. When the pirates had gained control, they could loot the ship at their leisure. Terrified travelers would lead the victorious pirates to their cabins, hoping to escape with their lives if they handed over their jewelry and other valuables.

BOARDING THE PRIZE

A pirate attack usually started with a cannon shot at the Spanish ship's mast or rigging, followed by some musket fire. As the ships drew closer, the pirates would toss over home-made "smoke bombs" and "grenades." Finally they threw grappling irons onto the Spanish rigging and hauled their own ship near enough to enable them to climb aboard.

◁ **No mercy**
The pirates inflicted vicious wounds on any Spaniards brave enough to fight.

Rigging

Anchor

Wooden casks were used to store water and salted meat.

The locked treasure chests were kept in the hold, often under armed guard.

Passenger's sleeping quarters.

The captain's Great Cabin.

6 SEE-THROUGH PIRATES

JOLLY ROGER

STEDE BONNET

EDWARD TEACH

BARTHOLOMEW ROBERTS

FLYING THE FLAG

Pirates used their flags to announce their identity and also to strike fear into the hearts of their victims in the hope that they would surrender without a fight. Some pirate flags were red, signifying that no one would be spared in battle. But by 1700, the black and white "skull and crossbones," often known as the Jolly Roger, had become by far the most popular design.

GRENADE   GRAPPLING HOOK

PIRATES IN PURSUIT

Before an attack, the pirates had to prepare their cannons, load their muskets and pistols, and tie their grappling hooks to the ends of long ropes. They also made "smoke-bombs" (earthenware pots filled with burning oil or sulfur) and "grenades" (small glass or iron containers filled with gunpowder). The grenades would explode on the enemy ship's deck, scattering sharp fragments and injuring the crew. Amid all the noise and confusion, the pirates would clamber aboard.

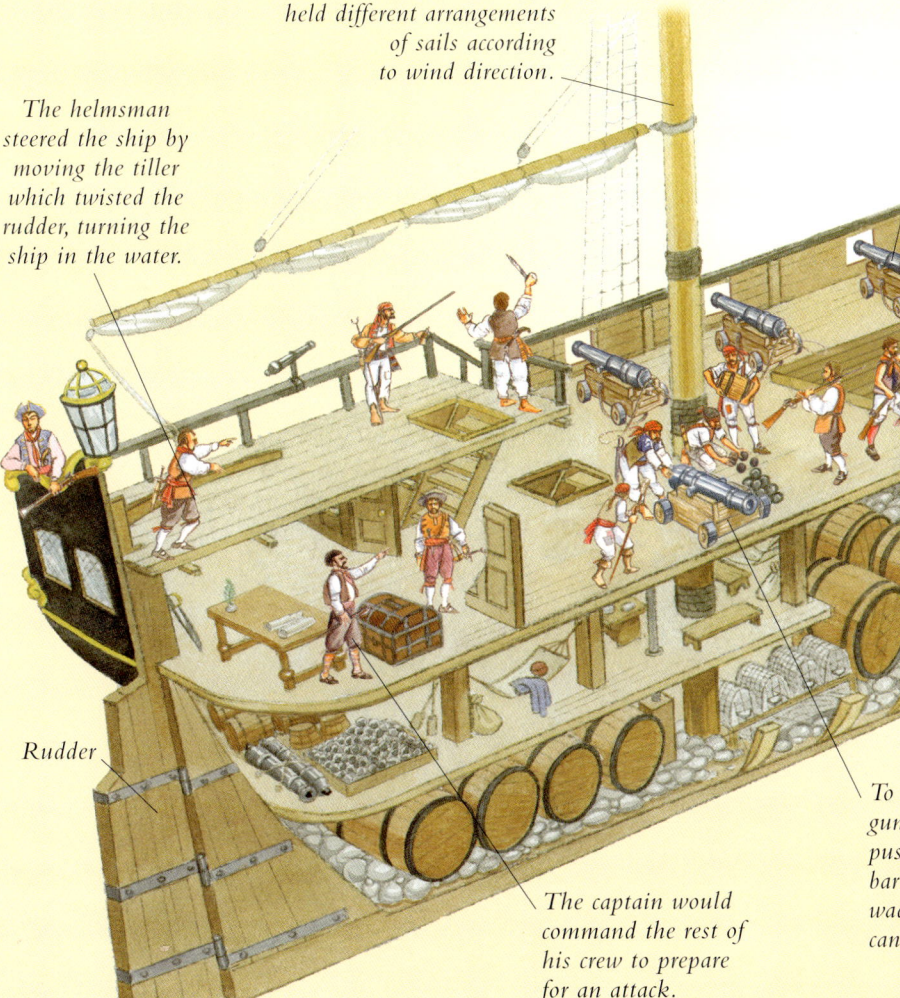

The sturdy mainmast held different arrangements of sails according to wind direction.

Heavy cannons were mounted on wheeled bases, to make them easier to aim and fire.

The helmsman steered the ship by moving the tiller which twisted the rudder, turning the ship in the water.

Anchor

Rudder

The captain would command the rest of his crew to prepare for an attack.

To load a cannon, gunpowder was pushed down the barrel, followed by wadding and a cannon ball or shot.

Ballast, stones, and barrels of water kept the ship steady in stormy seas.

◁ **A pirate flagship**
Pirate ships were laden with supplies, equipment, and weapons, as well as stolen treasure.

PIRATE ATTACK 9

PIRATE CREW

Pirates were extremely successful, partly because they were highly disciplined. Before the ship set sail, each man swore to keep the rules (or articles) of the ship by signing his name, or, if he could not write, making his mark. Pirates looked after each other, and the articles listed how much would be paid out to wounded men for the loss of limbs and other injuries. For instance, a man who lost an eye would be paid 100 pieces of eight, whereas a man who lost his right arm would usually receive 600 pieces of eight.

CALLING THE TUNE

Because the captain was elected by the crew, he had to command their respect. He had complete power over his men while they were chasing, or doing battle with, an enemy ship. But at other times the crew made the decisions. If they could not agree, they took a vote.

▽ **Everyone on deck!**
The pirate captain, accompanied by the quartermaster, addresses his crew before an attack.

The captain often wore expensive, colorful clothes made of silk or velvet.

The quartermaster, who enforced discipline, holds a cat-o'-nine-tails.

RULES ON BOARD SHIP

- Every man shall obey civil command; the captain shall have one full share and a half in all prizes; the master, carpenter, boatswain, and gunner shall have one share and a quarter.
- If any man shall offer to run away, or keep any secret from the company [the rest of the crew], he shall be maroon'd with one bottle of powder, one bottle of water, one small arm, and shot [ammunition].
- If any man shall lose a joint in time of an engagement he shall have 400 pieces of eight.
- If any man shall steel [steal] any thing in the company, or game, to the value of a piece of eight, he shall be maroon'd or shot.
- That man that shall strike another whilst these articles are in force, shall receive Moses's Law (that is, 40 stripes lacking one) on the bare back.
- That man that shall not keep his arms [weapons] clean, fit for an engagement [battle], or neglect his business [duty], shall be cut off from his share [of the loot], and suffer such other punishment as the captain and the company shall think fit.

SEE-THROUGH PIRATES

The quartermaster was the captain's second-in-command.

Muslin or silk cravats were favored by dandyish pirate captains.

Many pirates wore long, dark, loose-fitting jackets, with buttons.

Many pirates went barefoot, as leather shoes tended to slip on deck.

A flintlock pistol

Sea charts

A wide silk sash was often worn around the waist.

Quartermaster
The quartermaster punished the men if they were disobedient, usually by flogging them with a cat-o-nine-tails (a wooden stick holding nine knotted rope "tails"). He was also in charge of food and water supplies, of dividing up the treasure, and of paying the crew.

Pilot
The pilot was an expert navigator. He directed the ship's course using sea charts, a compass, and navigation instruments such as the astrolabe or backstaff. Both of these devices were used to measure the height of the sun or the North Star so that the ship's route could be plotted.

Captain
Generally chosen for his courage and leadership, a pirate captain would discipline anyone who disobeyed his orders during a chase or battle. He could also punish or execute prisoners. However, if he misused his authority, he could be ousted by his own crew.

Boatswain
The boatswain had to inspect the ship's sails and rigging each morning, and arrange repairs if necessary. He was also in charge of supplies (such as tar and tallow, a form of grease) and all deck activities, including weighing and dropping anchor, and raising and lowering the sails.

Master gunner
The master gunner was responsible for the ship's guns and ammunition. This included sifting the gunpowder to keep it dry and well mixed. In addition, he had to ensure that the cannonballs were free of rust, and that all weapons were in a good state of repair.

Ordinary seaman
Ordinary seamen had a dangerous, sometimes exciting, but often boring life in smelly conditions. Crew members included sailmakers and ship's cooks. Pirates were often injured in battle. If there was no surgeon on board, the ship's carpenter would remove shattered limbs.

PIRATE CREW 11

LIFE AT A PIRATE HAVEN

Between attacks, pirates would rest in safe ports or havens. In the 1600s many buccaneers had settled on Hispaniola and Tortuga, before moving on to Jamaica in the 1650s. But by 1717 one of the best-known pirate havens was New Providence Island in the Bahamas. Port Nassau, the island's capital, grew into a thriving town, teeming with merchants, traders, and buccaneers. The pirates might have been rich when they arrived, but they were usually poor when they left, having spent all their ill-gotten gains on drinking, gambling, and women.

THE PERFECT PIRATE HAVEN

New Providence Island was ideally situated to allow pirates to prey on Spanish ships that were passing through the narrow Florida Straits. It also had good anchorage for the pirates' vessels, and the surrounding waters were too shallow for the navy vessels that pursued them. By 1717 more than 500 pirates were using the island as a base.

PIRATE POINTS

How Port Royal was "punished for its sins"

- Britain took Jamaica from Spain in 1655 and the British asked the buccaneers to attack Spanish ships on their behalf. The Jamaican town of Port Royal became a well-known pirate haven.
- The Welsh buccaneer Henry Morgan (*see page 30*) was made Deputy Governor of Jamaica.
- In 1692 Port Royal was destroyed by an earthquake. Many believed that God had punished the town for its sins.

THE RISE AND FALL OF A HAVEN

When pirates first began to stop at Port Nassau, in around 1715, their main purpose was simply to resupply their ships with fresh water, timber, and meat. By 1718, however, Port Nassau was a flourishing town. Then a new English governor, Captain Woodes Rogers, arrived, with orders to rid New Providence of pirates.

▽ **Port Nassau in the early days**
The first New Providence pirates had to make their own timber shacks and tent dwellings.

A pirate ship rests at anchor in shallow water off of Port Nassau.

The men row ashore, bringing essential equipment from the ship.

Makeshift tents are rigged up, using old sails and ships' timbers.

12 SEE-THROUGH PIRATES

CAREENING AND CAULKING

In the warm Caribbean waters, seaweed and barnacles soon covered the bottom of pirate ships. Even worse, marine worms made holes in the hulls that could eventually sink them. Pirate crews therefore had to make regular stops to careen (beach and repair) their ships. The hull was thoroughly cleaned, and the gaps between the planks were caulked (filled with rope fibers and then sealed with hot pitch or tar). If pirates were unable to beach their ship, they would have to take it into very shallow water and stand on rafts to clean it.

PIRATE VICES

After long months at sea in a cramped, dirty ship, pirates were eager to enjoy themselves ashore. Some of them would spend thousands of pieces of eight in a single night—on beer, wine, rum, women, cards, and dice. Gambling for money was against the rules on many pirate ships, probably because it so often led to fights. But in the taverns of Port Nassau there were no such restrictions.

▷ **A nasty end**
Eight New Providence pirates refused to give up their wicked ways, and were duly hanged.

PIRATES DEFEATED

Captain Woodes Rogers arrived at Port Nassau in 1718, armed with warships, soldiers, and a Royal Pardon for the New Providence pirates if they became honest men. He soon succeeded in clearing the island of pirates.

▽ **Vulnerable to attack**
With their vessels beached, pirates had no means of escape from their enemies. They therefore favored secluded beaches for careening.

▽ **Friendly shipmates?**
A game of cards could soon lead to trouble, especially if the players were drinking.

The men often used a sharp-bladed cutting tool called an adz to chip off barnacles below the waterline.

LIFE AT A PIRATE HAVEN 15

PIRATE WEAPONS

Although pirates usually tried to frighten their victims into giving up without a fight, they were well prepared for battle. Their ships were armed with cannons, and the men were experienced at using boarding axes, cutlasses, daggers, pistols, muskets, and blunderbusses. In battle, most pirates carried at least two pistols because they could only be fired once before reloading. Many pirates also wore a baldrick, a kind of leather belt, holding spare powder charges for their pistols. Their lives often depended on their weapons so they took care to keep them clean and dry.

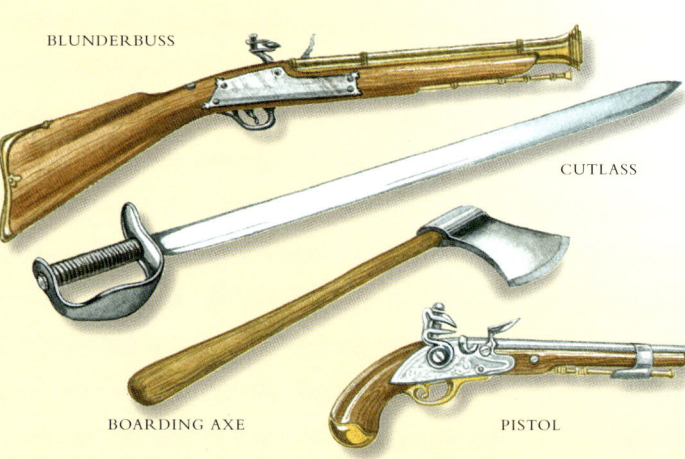

BLUNDERBUSS

CUTLASS

BOARDING AXE

PISTOL

CLOSE-COMBAT WEAPONS

Boarding axes helped the pirates climb the high wooden sides of the ships. Once aboard, daggers and short, broad cutlasses were the main weapons, because longer swords could easily get caught in the rigging. The blunderbuss was used at close range because its funnel-shaped barrel gave it a wide but unreliable aim in comparison with the pistol's long narrow barrel.

SHIP'S CANNONS

A typical pirate sloop carried four-pounder cannons mounted on four-wheeled bases. They could fire chainshot and barshot to damage the enemy ship's rigging and sails, roundshot (or cannon balls) to splinter the hull, and grapeshot to cut down men at close range.

▽ **Firing a cannon**
Gunpowder, wadding, and shot were pushed down the barrel. Then the fuse was lit. When it fired, the cannon sprang back with great force.

PIRATE POINTS

☠ **The origin of "a flash in the pan"**
- This well-known phrase comes from a musket or pistol misfire. A spark from the flint lit the gunpowder, but there was only a flash and the lead ball was not actually fired.
- This might happen if there was too little powder in the pan, or if too coarse a grade of powder had been used, or the touch hole was blocked.

Ropes prevented the cannon sliding too far back.

The barrel had to be cleaned with a sponge after each firing.

Fuse

SEE-THROUGH PIRATES

FLINTLOCK PISTOLS

Because they were light to carry, flintlock pistols were often used at close range. However they were useless if the gunpowder was damp. Pirates therefore had to keep their powder dry in horns or leather flasks with metal lids. In addition, reloading flintlock pistols took a long time. For this reason many pirates would just fire them once and then use the pistol butt as a club instead.

How to fire a flintlock pistol

1. Check the flint (a small, sharp piece of rock that could be struck against steel to produce a spark). If it is dull, replace it.
2. Bring the lock to the half-cock position. Pour in just enough powder to fill the outer half of the flash pan, away from the touch hole.
3. Blow away from the lock any grains of loose powder.
4. Turn the barrel upward, and pour in some powder.
5. Insert a lead ball into the barrel.
6. Insert some wadding (a small piece of cloth) into the barrel.
7. Using the fingertips only (in case the pistol accidentally goes off), take the rammer from beneath the barrel and use it to ram home both the wadding and the charge.
8. Put the rammer back in its place below the barrel.
9. Raise the lock into the firing position.
10. Firmly pull the trigger with your right forefinger. This lowers the lock, which scrapes the flint down a piece of steel, showering sparks on to the priming powder. This, in turn, ignites the main charge, firing the pistol.

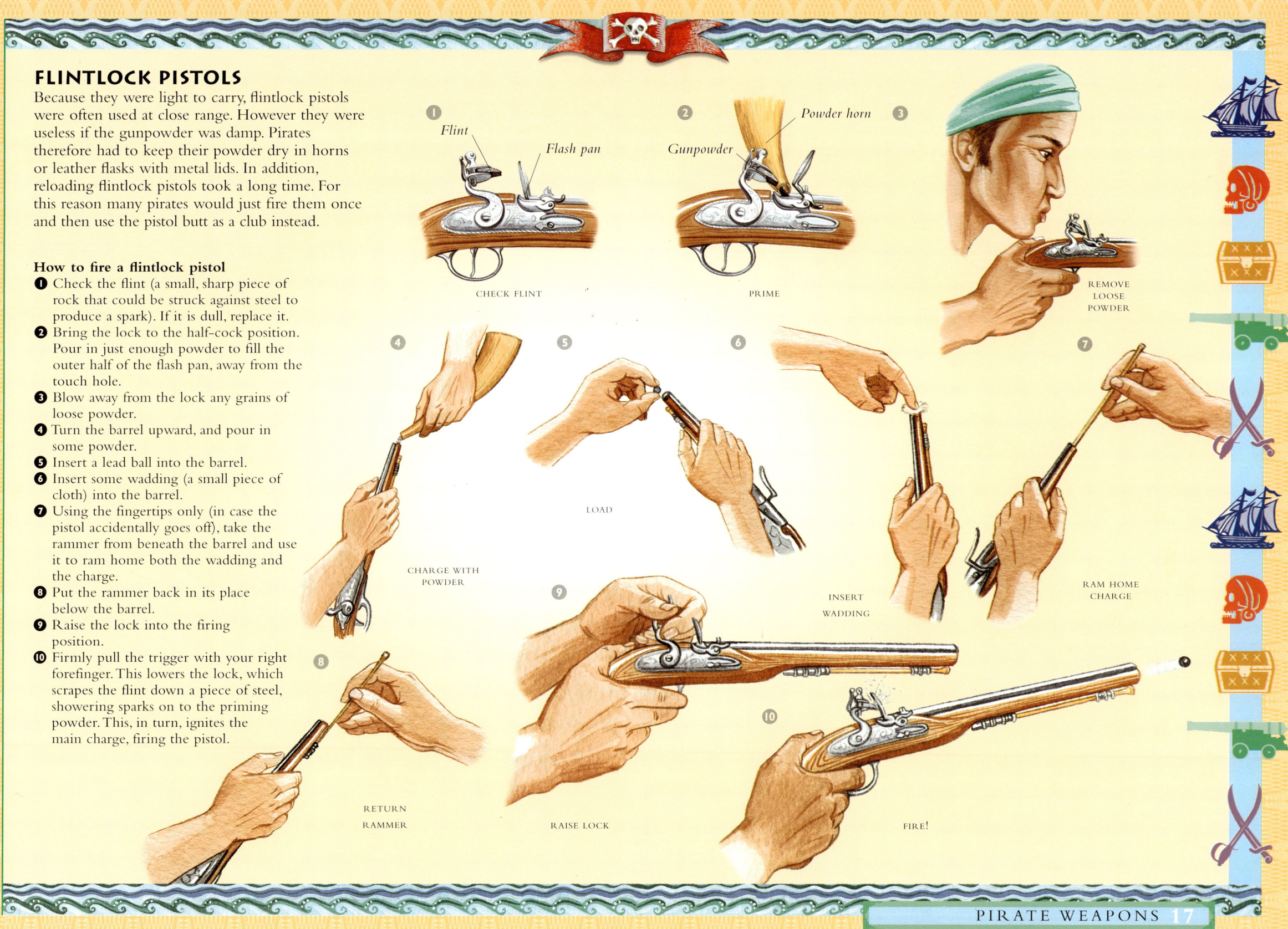

PIRATE WEAPONS 17

PIRATE PUNISHMENTS

Pirates used many different punishments, both to discipline their own men and to torture prisoners in order to extract information from them. Sometimes a wrongdoer had to "run the gauntlet." This meant that he had to strip naked and run round the deck. Each pirate that he passed would hit him with a knotted rope or would stab him with a hook, needle, or knife. Alternatively, for a relatively minor offence such as starting a fight, a man might be "ducked." For this punishment, he was tied to one end of a long spar and was then dunked into the ocean for hours on end while the ship sailed along.

MAROONED!

ALONE AND ABANDONED

A pirate who robbed or betrayed another pirate was marooned—left on a deserted island with only a bottle of water, a musket, gunpowder, and some shot. When his supplies ran out, he might try to survive by catching fish. A few fortunate "marooners" were rescued by passing ships. One of them, a Scottish sailor named Alexander Selkirk (on whom Daniel Defoe based his book *Robinson Crusoe*, published in 1710), survived on an island near Chile for more than four years. But in most cases being marooned was equivalent to a death sentence.

STUCK IN A SUGAR BARREL

For this punishment, the victim was pushed into a barrel that had last been used to hold sticky sugar. The lid was jammed on and then the top of the barrel was covered with a thick blanket, which meant that it became hotter and hotter inside.

LASHED WITH THE "CAT"

Flogging was carried out in front of the entire crew. The victim was stripped to the waist and tied to a grating. Then the quartermaster lashed the man's back with the cat-o'nine-tails. Salt and vinegar were later rubbed into the man's wounds to stop them from getting infected.

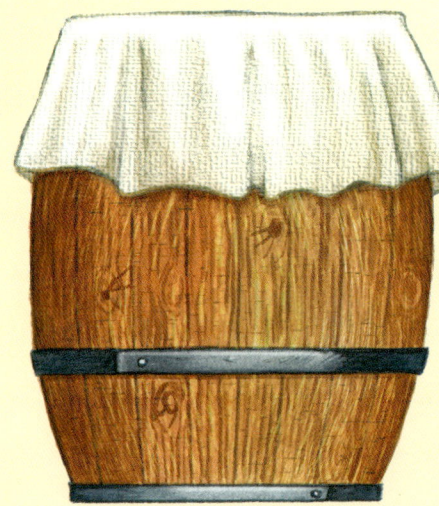

◁ **Hellish heat**
The wrongdoer was left sweating in the dark for several hours, barely able to breathe, with only cockroaches and rats for company.

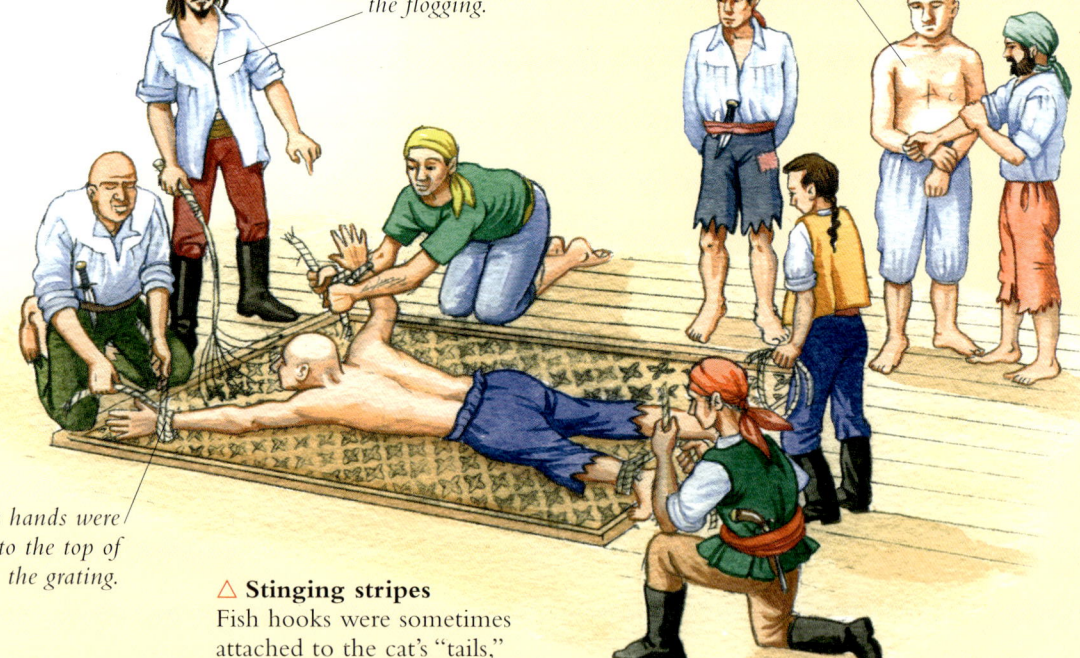

It was always the quartermaster who carried out the flogging.

The whole crew watched, each man knowing that he could be next.

The man's hands were firmly tied to the top of the grating.

△ **Stinging stripes**
Fish hooks were sometimes attached to the cat's "tails," making the punishment even more painful.

KEEL-HAULING

When a man was keel-hauled, his hands and feet were tied with a rope and then he was hauled under the ship, from one side to the other. The barnacles on the underside of the ship scraped his skin, leaving it raw and bleeding. This cruel punishment dated back to the days of the ancient Greeks.

▽ **A naval tradition**
Flogging and keel-hauling were both used in the British Navy and, in fact, pirates used these punishments far less than sailors. Keel-hauling had been abolished by the eighteenth century and flogging was outlawed in 1886.

PIRATE POINTS

☠ **Not many pirates walked the plank**
- Contrary to popular belief, pirates seldom forced their victims to walk the plank. More often, they were simply thrown overboard.
- Alternatively, the wrongdoer might first be "stitched up" (sewn into a piece of old sailcloth) or "weighed down" (tied to a heavy weight, such as a dead body).

△ **Ankle rings**
The metal rings would press painfully on the prisoner's ankles.

LOCKED IN LEG IRONS

Pirates who were found guilty of an offence could be sent down to the ship's hold, which acted as a temporary prison, and there "clapped in irons." Even worse, they might be locked in leg irons on the ship's deck, and left to suffer in the blazing heat or the howling wind and rain.

BURNING

This was a particularly brutal punishment, for which the victim's arms and legs were first securely tied. Pieces of rope were then placed between the man's fingers and toes, and lit. George Lowther, a pirate in the Caribbean in the early 1720s, famously used this method of torture to force plundered ships' crew members to tell him where their treasure was hidden.

▽ **Searing pain**
The rope fibers would start smoldering, burning the victim's hands and feet.

A strong rope was required for keel-hauling.

The victim often died immediately from drowning, or later from infected wounds.

The hull was usually covered with slimy weed and razor-sharp barnacles.

The unraveled rope fibers used for this punishment were known as oakum.

This captive would soon be begging for mercy.

PIRATE PUNISHMENTS 21

LIFE AT SEA

Attacking treasure ships was dangerous and exciting, and pirate havens offered plenty of illicit pleasures. But the rest of the time, when they were simply sailing the seas, pirates' lives were pretty miserable. Their sleeping quarters were cramped, they had few washing facilities, and their ships usually smelled of bilge water, tar, and rat droppings. There was plenty of work to be done, but the tasks were tedious and tiring. Many of the pirates tried to escape the boredom of daily life by getting drunk on rum and looted wine and brandy. They also passed the time by singing work songs known as sea shanties, dancing jigs, and playing the fiddle and the concertina.

DAILY CHORES

Pirates often had to work very hard. For instance, everyday they used bilge pumps to clear out any water that had collected down below in the ship's hold. It was pumped up on to the deck and drained out through the scuppers (drain holes at the sides). Other daily chores included furling and mending the sails, swabbing the decks, caulking the planks (filling and sealing any gaps), and keeping a lookout for other ships or land.

Furling (rolling up) the sails meant climbing high up the rigging.

Decks had to be swabbed every day, otherwise they became dangerously slippery.

PIRATE POINTS

 The personal habits of pirates
- There were no toilets on board. Pirates used a hole in the front of the ship, from which the waste dropped into the sea, or they relieved themselves over the side.
- According to ship's rules, candles and lanterns had to be put out by eight o'clock. Pirates usually slept in hammocks below deck.

▽ **At work and play**
Lively music could help to take the pirates' minds off of their boring, repetitive duties.

The lookout used a telescope to search for ships to plunder.

 SEE-THROUGH PIRATES

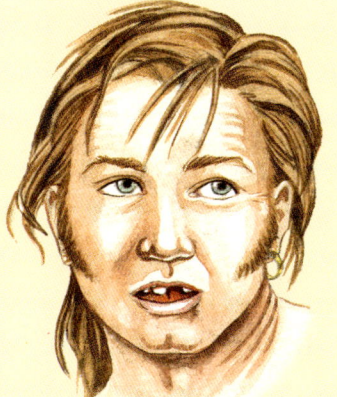

A MAN WITH SCURVY

DISEASES AND INJURIES

The most common illness at sea was scurvy, which was caused by a lack of vitamin C (found in fresh fruits and vegetables). Victims suffered bleeding gums and often lost their teeth. Yellow fever was another danger. After a fever lasting several days, pirates either recovered or died. But the most frequent problem was infected wounds. If gangrene got into the wound, it rotted the surrounding flesh and the ship's doctor had to remove the limb.

PIRATE POINTS

 How pirates got fresh food

- Sea turtles were caught and sometimes kept on deck or in the hold. Their meat was barbecued over a smoky fire. Pirates also ate soft-shelled turtle eggs.
- Goats were sometimes kept for their milk and hens provided eggs (or "cackle-fruit," as they were known).
- Fresh fish could almost always be caught. In the Caribbean, pirates found a ready supply of tuna, mullet, and dolphin.

TAKING A SOUNDING

MEASURING SEA DEPTH

To take a sounding, the sailing master used a long, weighted rope, with evenly spaced fabric ties along its length. When the lead weight touched the bottom, he looked at the fabric markers to calculate how deep the water was.

In addition, the hollow lead weight was filled with sticky fat. The sailing master would check what type of sand and pebbles were sticking to the end of the weight, and this would help him work out the ship's probable location.

Pirates drank from pewter tankards and ate off pewter plates.

Most pirates ate greedily, so mealtimes were often messy.

△ **A meal on board**
Pirates usually had their meals at a big wooden table in the captain's Great Cabin.

Turtle or chicken stew was sometimes on the menu.

FOOD AND DRINK

Much of the time, pirates lived on dried or salted fish and meat, dried beans, and ship's biscuits. Known as "hard tack," ship's biscuits were made of flour and water that had been baked rock-hard. They were very long-lasting but were usually full of weevils and maggots. As for drinks, fresh water soon turned foul, so ships had to carry plenty of ale for the crew. Pirates also expected a daily swig of rum (which was also known as "kill-devil" or "rumbullion"), a sweet-tasting alcohol that was made from molasses. And rum could be used to make "bumboo," a mixture of rum, water, sugar, and nutmeg.

LIFE AT SEA 23

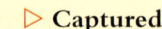

CAPTURE AND TRIAL

By the end of the seventeenth century there was great public outrage at the vast amount of piracy that was occurring in the Spanish Main. Pirate attacks were becoming ever more frequent and costly, and the British government finally decided to take firm action. Royal Navy ships, under the command of men like Robert Maynard and Chaloner Ogle, were sent out to hunt down and capture well-known pirates such as Edward Teach (*see page 30*) and Bartholomew Roberts (*see page 31*). Many pirates were offered pardons, but those who refused to give up piracy could expect little mercy.

PIRATES ON TRIAL

Until the 1700s, captured pirates were sent to prison in London. Later, they were tried in the places where they had committed their crimes. Their old haven, Port Royal, thus became the scene of both their trial and their execution. The mass trials seldom lasted more than two days—and usually ended with multiple death sentences.

THE NAVY TO THE RESCUE

Naval ships protected convoys of merchant ships from pirate raids, and they also went into battle against pirate vessels. In most cases, the pirates were defeated because the navy had larger ships, with more guns. In addition, the pirates were pursued by pirate hunters in privately owned vessels, who were hoping to win a reward for their capture.

▷ **Captured**
Once bound in chains, the previously savage pirates were helpless and simply had to await their fate.

▽ **Unequal contest**
A heavily armed, three-masted naval frigate would soon triumph over a single-masted pirate sloop.

JUDGE AND GROUP OF PIRATES AT A TRIAL.

24 SEE-THROUGH PIRATES

WARSHIPS AND FRIGATES

The Royal Navy's vessels ranged from relatively small frigates (like the 20-gun *Greyhound*, which pursued the pirate Edward Low) to large warships, such as Chaloner Ogle's 50-gun HMS *Swallow*, which triumphed over Bartholomew Roberts (see page 31). Frigates were small, fast ships with fewer than 50 guns, like the example below (based on HMS *Pandora*). By the 1720s, the ships sent out to pursue the pirates tended to be bigger and better armed than those sailed by the pirates. Pirates also sailed a variety of vessels, including stolen warships and merchant ships, but more commonly small sloops. For instance, Stede Bonnet (see page 30) began his career as a pirate in the 10-gun sloop *Revenge*. He bought the vessel in Carolina, and paid 70 seamen to be his crew.

▽ **Inside a frigate**
Frigates were well-constructed three-masted vessels, with comfortable living quarters for the captain and his officers.

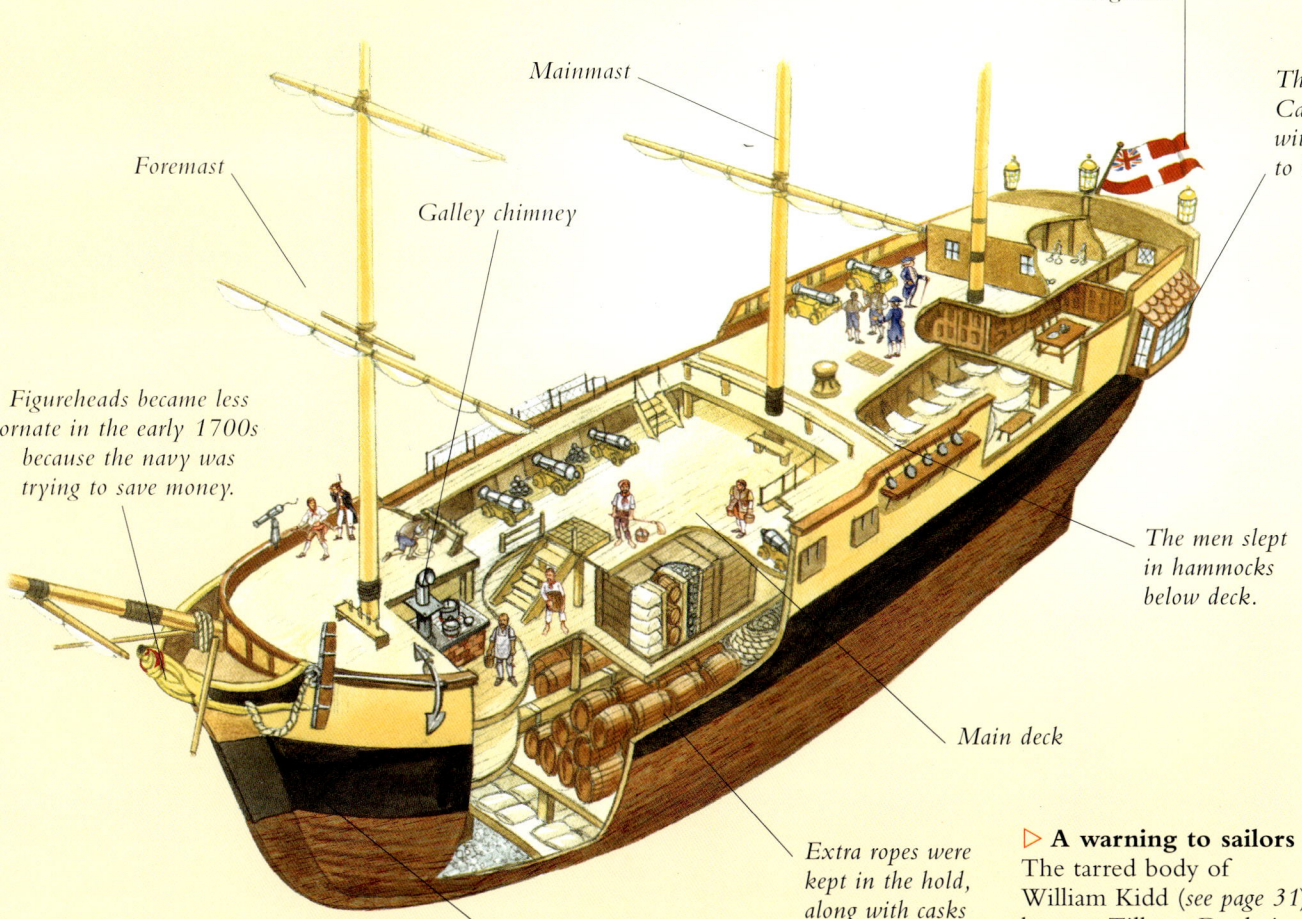

Figureheads became less ornate in the early 1700s because the navy was trying to save money.

Foremast

Galley chimney

Mainmast

The Union Jack flag proclaimed the frigate's British allegiance.

The captain's Great Cabin was very airy, with glass windows to let in light.

The men slept in hammocks below deck.

Main deck

Anchor

Extra ropes were kept in the hold, along with casks of water and salted meat.

▷ **A warning to sailors**
The tarred body of William Kidd (see page 31) hung at Tilbury Dock, in England, for many years.

PIRATE POINTS

☠ **When Caribbean pirates were executed**
- In 1716, Jack Rackham (see page 31) and nine pirates were executed in Kingston, Jamaica.
- In 1718, 13 of Edward Teach's (see page 30) men were put to death in Williamsburg, Virginia; Stede Bonnet (see page 30) and 30 pirates got the death penalty in Charleston, North Carolina; and eight pirates were hanged in New Providence Island.
- In 1723, Charles Harris and 25 pirates were executed in Newport, Rhode Island.
- In 1726, William Fly and two pirates were put to death in Boston, Massachusetts.

HUNG IN CHAINS

After execution by hanging, the pirate's body was chained into an iron cage, washed by three tides, and then preserved with a coating of tar. It was hoped that this gruesome sight, when left hanging at the entrance to a port, would discourage others from becoming pirates.

CAPTURE AND TRIAL   27

THE TRUE STORY OF THE WHYDAH

The *Whydah* is the only known shipwreck to be recognized as an authentic pirate vessel. Allegedly laden with treasure from 53 ships, the *Whydah* was caught in a fierce storm off Cape Cod, Massachusetts, and quickly sank within sight of the beach in 1717. Only two of the crew members survived. One of them, Thomas Davis, testified in court that the *Whydah*'s booty included 180 bags of gold and silver. Since 1984, Barry Clifford and a team of divers have been recovering weapons, coins, jewelry, and other assorted objects from the site of the wreck.

THE CAPTAIN

"Black Sam" Bellamy left England in the 1700s to become a privateer, raiding Spanish ships in the West Indies. When the war against Spain ended in 1713, he became a pirate. He is said to have cut a very dashing figure, wearing a velvet coat, silver-buckled shoes, a sword slung on his hip, and with his dark hair tied back with a black satin bow.

BLACK SAM BELLAMY

BELLAMY'S FIRST SHIPS

By May 1716, Sam Bellamy had become the captain of the 10-gun pirate sloop *Mary Anne* and soon began preying on cargo ships in the Caribbean. His first prize was the *Sultana*, an English man-of-war, which he took as his flagship. The next victim was an Irish merchant ship, carrying a welcome supply of ham, butter, and cheese. With his five-vessel fleet, Black Sam is thought to have looted more than 50 ships in the Virgin Islands that winter. Between raids, he and his men returned to their base in the Virgin Islands to drink and celebrate.

▽ **An easy target**
Bellamy's crew struck lucky when they raided a group of salvors recovering treasure from Spanish wrecks.

PIRATE POINTS

☠ **The life and times of Black Sam**

- Bellamy is believed to have grown up in Devonshire, England.
- He was known as the "Prince of Pirates" because he could be surprisingly generous to his victims. For instance, when he found a stolen sloop, the *St Michael*, too slow for his needs, he returned it to its crew!
- Bellamy was active in the Caribbean at the same time as Edward Teach (*see page 30*). The two pirates may even have met.

THE WHYDAH

A 300-tonne, 18-gun three-master, the *Whydah* first left London in 1715 as a slave ship under the command of Lawrence Prince. Her crew exchanged English cloth, liquor, tools, and weapons for West African slaves, then traded the slaves in Jamaica for gold, silver, sugar, and indigo (a blue dye). When Sam Bellamy captured the *Whydah* she was on her way back to London, laden with treasure—a rich prize. Black Sam made the *Whydah* his new flagship and transferred another ten guns to her deck. With 28 guns, she was now well enough armed to take on any merchant vessel.

△ **Pursued by pirates**
After leaving Jamaica in February 1717, the *Whydah* was captured by Bellamy near the Bahamas.

DISCOVERY OF THE WHYDAH

In 1984, Barry Clifford's team of divers found a ship's cannon and a blackened coin. The following year they recovered the ship's bell, inscribed "Whydah Gally, 1716," and the discovery of the *Whydah* became official. Since then they have retrieved from the wreck more than 2,000 Spanish gold coins, as well as knives, pistols, musket balls, tableware, navigation equipment, jewelry (much of it apparently taken from African slaves), and clothing. One of their most striking discoveries has been a pirate's leg bone, still in its silk stocking, with a small, black leather shoe.

△ **Determined divers**
Retrieving heavy objects, such as cannons, can be both difficult and risky for Barry Clifford's team of divers.

▷ **The *Whydah* meets her end**
In April 1717, amid dense fog, lashing rain, and 30-foot (10-meter) waves, the *Whydah* struck a sandbar off Cape Cod.

PIRATE POINTS

More about the wreck of the *Whydah*

- In April 1717, the *Whydah* was heading for Richmond Island, off the Maine coast. But Bellamy decided to change the fleet's course for Cape Cod, perhaps because he wanted to visit his mistress, Maria Hallet, who lived there.
- About 30–50 members of Bellamy's crew are thought to have been former slaves who were offered freedom if they became pirates.
- 144 men died when the *Whydah* sank suddenly in a violent storm, including Bellamy himself.

THE TRUE STORY OF THE WHYDAH

ROGUES' GALLERY

Brave, foolish, swaggering, bloodthirsty, greedy, cunning, vain, and even sometimes surprisingly courteous, pirates have certainly earned their place in history. Their colorful deeds have inspired the makers of Hollywood films, as well as writers such as Robert Louis Stevenson, author of *Treasure Island*, and J. M. Barrie, author of *Peter Pan*. Here are some of the real-life Captain Hooks and Long John Silvers who sailed the seas and looted treasure during the Golden Age of piracy.

SIR HENRY MORGAN

SIR HENRY MORGAN

Born in Wales, Henry Morgan (ca.1635–1688) sailed to the Caribbean as a young man. He joined the buccaneers on Tortuga, took part in several successful raids on Spanish ships, and subsequently became a wealthy plantation owner in Jamaica. The Governor of Jamaica then asked Morgan to become an English privateer. With the Governor's permission, Morgan began attacking Spanish settlements in South America, including Puerto Principe in Cuba, Maracaibo in Venezuela, and Panama. King Charles II of England was so delighted by Morgan's victories against the Spanish that in 1674 he made him Deputy Governor of Jamaica.

STEDE BONNET

Stede Bonnet (ca.1688–1718), a retired army major, was a rich, middle-aged plantation owner in Barbados when he suddenly shocked his friends and neighbors by leaving to become a pirate. He bought a 10-gun sloop called the *Revenge* and captured a few vessels off the Virginian coast, but due to his inexperience achieved only limited success. He was briefly befriended by Edward Teach, who was very amused by Bonnet's gentlemanly manners. He was hanged at Charleston, Carolina, in 1718.

HENRY AVERY

Sometimes also known as John Every, Henry Avery (1665–1728) first went to sea as a sailor with the Royal Navy. While privateering against the Spanish, he and the crew mutinied and became pirates. In 1695, Avery mounted his most famous raid—on the Moghul emperor's treasure ship, the *Gang-i-Sawai*, which was returning across the Red Sea to India from Mecca. The wealthy pilgrims on board were robbed of their riches, including half a million coins. Avery is believed to have died penniless in England, having been tricked out of his wealth by merchants.

EDWARD TEACH

Edward Teach (ca.1680–1718), an Englishman, was better known as "Blackbeard." He wore his long, wild hair and beard in twisted tails and, before going into battle, would light smoldering fuses under his hat. Armed with six pistols, a sword, and a cutlass, he was a terrifying sight. He was a privateer in Jamaica before he turned to piracy. Having captured his 40-gun flagship, the *Queen Anne's Revenge*, from the French, he began terrorizing the North American coast. However, his career as a pirate captain lasted only two years. In 1718, a British naval officer, Lieutenant Robert Maynard, caught up with Blackbeard off the coast of Carolina, and killed him in a fierce fight.

EDWARD TEACH (BLACKBEARD)

PIRATE POINTS

☠ Fearsome facts about Edward Teach

- If a prisoner refused to give Blackbeard a ring, he simply took it—by chopping the prisoner's finger off.
- Once while drinking with his first mate, Israel Hands, Blackbeard suddenly fired his pistol under the table, deliberately wounding Hands in the knee. (The first mate was lame for the rest of his life.)
- In his final duel with Robert Maynard, the pirate is said to have been shot five times and wounded 20 times.
- Maynard cut off Blackbeard's head and hung it from the spar at the front of his ship.

30 SEE-THROUGH PIRATES

WILLIAM KIDD

WILLIAM KIDD
Born in Scotland, the unfortunate William Kidd (ca.1645–1701) was sent as a privateer to the Indian Ocean. His mission was to attack French ships because England was at war with France. However, he spent several months without capturing a single ship, and his men threatened to mutiny. Finally he attacked an Indian-owned ship, the *Quedah Merchant*, which was under French protection, making it a legal target. Nevertheless, Kidd was later found guilty of piracy and executed in 1701.

JOHN RACKHAM
John Rackham (?–1720) was known as "Calico Jack," because he often wore striped calico coats and breeches. He served as quartermaster aboard Charles Vane's ship, the *Treasure*, until the crew voted to make him captain. In the Bahamas he met an Irishwoman, Anne Bonny, who willingly left her husband and joined his crew. They were later joined by Mary Read, and the three of them continued to plunder ships together until they were captured by the Royal Navy in 1720.

PIRATE POINTS

☠ Disturbing details about William Kidd
- In a fit of temper, Kidd once threw a wooden bucket at a crew member. It broke the man's skull and he died.
- Kidd buried much of the treasure from the *Quedah Merchant* on Gardiner's Island, near New York.
- The French documents from the *Quedah Merchant*, which would have proved him innocent, strangely disappeared during Kidd's trial and were rediscovered years after his death.

BARTHOLOMEW ROBERTS (BLACK BART)

BARTHOLOMEW ROBERTS
The Welshman Bartholomew Roberts (1682–1722), who was also known as "Black Bart," was both handsome and brave. He wore a crimson silk waistcoat, a gold chain with a jeweled cross, and a hat with a scarlet plume. Unusually for a pirate, Roberts never drank and encouraged his men to pray. He is said to have captured nearly 400 ships in the Caribbean and off the coast of West Africa. Roberts was finally killed in a battle with the naval ship HMS *Swallow* (see page 27).

WOMEN PIRATES
Historically, almost all pirates were men, although three women also achieved fame as "sea-robbers." Grace O'Malley, an Irish noblewoman, attacked English ships off western Ireland from the 1560s to the 1580s. She retired in 1593, when Queen Elizabeth I of England pardoned her. Much later, in the 1700s, another Irishwoman followed in Grace's footsteps. Anne Bonny, the daughter of a wealthy Irish lawyer, married a sailor and went to New Providence Island. There she met and fell in love with John Rackham. Dressed as a man, she sailed with Calico Jack's crew, and took part in many raids on Spanish treasure ships. Around 1717 they captured a sloop on which Mary Read was sailing.

Born in England, Mary had been brought up as a boy in order to claim a family inheritance. She had previously been in the army and had sailed with pirates, and she was happy to join Rackham and Bonny. In 1720, their ship was captured by a British privateer off of Jamaica, with the two women putting up the strongest fight. Rackham was hanged, but the court decided not to execute Bonny and Read because they were both pregnant. Mary Read died of a fever in prison. Nothing more is known of Anne Bonny, who famously said to Rackham: "Had you fought like a man, you need not have been hanged like a dog."

ANNE BONNY   MARY READ   GRACE O'MALLEY

GLOSSARY AND INDEX

adz A sharp tool with a blade at one end. Used by pirates to shape wood and to scrape barnacles off ships' hulls.

anchorage A place near the shore where the water is the right depth for ships to anchor safely.

ballast Heavy material, such as stones or water barrels, that was carried by a ship to keep it steady in the water.

barnacle A small, sharp-edged shellfish, which collects in large numbers on rocks and ships' hulls.

bilge pump A pump used to remove the dirty water that collects in the bottom of a ship.

bireme Literally translated as a "two-er"; a type of galley used by the ancient Romans, which required two rows of oarsmen.

butt, pistol The wooden handle of a pistol.

calico A type of heavy cotton cloth.

careen To take a ship ashore for cleaning and repairs.

cat-o'-nine-tails A whip of nine knotted rope cords fastened to a handle, used to punish crew members on ships.

caulk To fill gaps between a ship's planks with rope fibers and then coat the repairs with tar to make them waterproof.

convoy A group of ships or vehicles traveling together for protection.

doubloon A gold coin used in Spain and the Caribbean. One doubloon was worth about seven weeks' pay for an ordinary sailor in the 1700s.

frigate A small, fast-moving, three-masted naval ship, with fewer than 50 guns, often used to protect other ships.

galleon A large sailing ship of the type used by the Spanish to carry treasure from the New World in the sixteenth and seventeenth centuries.

galley (1) A shallow-bottomed warship, with sails and oars. (2) A ship's kitchen.

grappling iron A four-pronged metal hook, attached to a rope, which was used to gain hold of another ship and to pull it alongside before it was boarded.

hold The storage area at the bottom of a ship.

hull The outer shell of a ship.

junk A large, flat-bottomed wooden sailing ship used by the Chinese.

manacles A pair of iron rings, joined by a chain, used to fasten the hands or feet of prisoners.

paddle steamer A steamship that is pushed forward by a pair of large paddle wheels. Unlike the Chinese pirates' sailing vessels, nineteenth-century naval paddle steamers were capable of sailing directly against the wind. This ensured their victory over the pirates of Southeast Asia.

peso A silver Spanish coin; also known as a "piece of eight," because it could be torn into pieces in order to make change. Two pieces of eight were enough to buy a cow in the 1700s.

pewter A mixture of lead and tin used to make the hard-wearing dishes and cups used by pirates.

rudder A blade at the back of a ship that swings from side to side to change the direction in which the ship moves.

salvor Someone who salvages (or recovers) what is left—for example from a shipwreck.

sandbar A stretch of sand formed by moving currents. Ships can easily run aground on sandbars.

ship's biscuit A long-lasting biscuit, made from flour and water, eaten by ships' crews.

sloop A fast, single-masted sailing vessel.

spar A thick pole, used on a ship to support sails or ropes.

swab To clean a ship's decks.

tallow Hard animal fat, used to make candles.

tavern An inn or drinking den.

tiller A long handle attached to a ship's rudder. Used by the helmsman to steer the ship.

trireme Literally translated as a "three-er"; a type of galley used by the ancient Romans, which required three rows of oarsmen.

wadding A small piece of cloth placed in the barrel of a pistol or cannon before loading shot.

A
adz 15, 32
Alexander the Great 3
articles 10
astrolabe 11
Avery, Henry 30
axe 16

B
backstaff 11
Bahamas 4, 12, 29, 31
ballast 9, 32
Barbary corsair 3
Bellamy, "Black Sam" 28, 29
bilge pump 22, 32
bireme 3, 32
blunderbuss 16
boatswain 10, 11
Bonnet, Stede 9, 27, 30
Bonny, Anne 31
British (Royal) Navy 3, 21, 24, 27, 30, 31
buccaneer 5, 12, 30
burning 21

C
Caesar, Julius 3
cannon 6, 11, 16, 29
captain 6, 10, 11, 27, 28, 30, 31
careening 15, 32
Caribbean 4, 5, 6, 15, 21, 23, 27, 28, 30, 31, 32
carpenter 10, 11
cat-o'-nine-tails 10, 11, 18, 32
caulking 15, 22, 32
Charles II, King 30
Clifford, Barry 28, 29
Columbus, Christopher 4
cutlass 6, 16, 30

D
dagger 16
Davis, Thomas 28
disease 23
doubloon 5, 32

Drake, Francis 5
drink 15, 23, 28
ducking 18

E
Elizabeth I, Queen 31

F
Ferdinand, King 4
figurehead 27
flag 9, 27
flogging 18, 21
Fly, William 27
food 23
frigate 24, 27, 32

G
galleon 4, 6, 32
galley 3, 9, 32
gambling 15
Gang-i-Sawai 30
grappling hook iron 6, 16, 32
Great Cabin 23, 27
Greyhound 27
gunpowder 11, 16, 17, 18

H
Hands, Israel 30
hanging 15, 27, 30, 31
Harris, Charles 27
haven 12, 22, 24
helmsman 9, 32
Hispaniola 4, 5, 12

I
injuries 6, 10, 11, 23

J
Jamaica 4, 5, 12, 27, 29, 30, 31
Jolly Roger 9
junk 3, 32

K
keel-hauling 21
Kidd, William 27, 31

L
leg irons 21
longship 3
lookout 4, 22
Low, Edward 27
Lowther, George 21

M
manacles 24, 32
man-of-war 28
Mary Anne 28
master gunner 10, 11
Maynard, Lieutenant Robert 24, 30
mending 22
merchant vessel 3, 24, 27, 28, 29
Morgan, Sir Henry 12, 30
Moses's Law 10
music 22
musket 16, 18

N
New Providence Island 12, 15, 27, 31
New World 4, 5

O
oakum 21, 32
Ogle, Chaloner 24, 27
l'Olonnais, François 5
O'Malley, Grace 31

P
paddle steamer 3, 32
pardon 15, 24
peso 5, 32
Phillips, John 10
piece of eight 5, 10, 15, 32
pilot 11
pistol 11, 16, 17, 30, 32
Pompey the Great 3
Port Nassau 12, 15
Port Royal 12, 24
Prince, Lawrence 29
privateer 5, 28, 30
punishment 10, 11, 12, 18, 21, 32

Q
quartermaster 10, 11, 18, 31
Quedah Merchant 31
Queen Anne's Revenge 30

R
Rackham, John/Jack 27, 31
Read, Mary 31
Revenge 10, 27
rigging 22
Roberts, Bartholomew 5, 9, 24, 27, 31
Rogers, Captain Woodes 12, 15
rudder 9, 32
rum 15, 23
running the gauntlet 18

S
St Michael 28
sea shanty 22
ship's biscuit 23, 32
shot 16, 18, 32
sloop 4, 6, 16, 24, 27, 28, 31, 32
smoke bomb 6
sounding 23
Spanish Main 4, 24
sugar barrel 18
Sultana 28
swabbing 22, 32
Swallow, HMS 27, 31

T
Teach, Edward 9, 24, 27, 30
tiller 9, 32
Tortuga 4, 5, 12, 30
treasure 4, 5, 6, 9, 11, 21, 22, 28, 29, 30, 31, 32
Treasure 31
trireme 3, 32

W
wadding 16, 17, 32
walking the plank 21
warship 6, 27, 32
weapons 6, 10, 11, 16
Whydah 28, 29

Y
yardarm 18